From Small Beginnings ...

So what is this 'Dartmoor Letterboxing' all about then? This is a question which has been addressed to us so many times after people have discovered that we, as a family, are 'letterboxers'.

'What ¿
'Where do
'How do y
keener one:
booklet is
curious folk
give it a go

but who need that initial injection of knowledge
something we regard as an adventure.

Our interest in the hobby, for that is what it is to most folk, began after our daughter attended a school camp near Haytor, on Eastern Dartmoor. The teachers took the children on a short letterbox walk and when our daughter returned home she enthusiastically showed us the attractive and interesting letterbox 'stamps' that she had collected that day. Consequently we decided to give 'letterboxing' a try and have enjoyed it ever since.

The hobby is best described as being like a very large, never-ending, game of 'Hide and Seek' – someone hides a weatherproof box containing a rubber stamp and a 'visitor's book' and you have to find it ... it really is that simple! Except there are rather a lot of them and they are hidden all over the moor. Although it is possible to find them just by looking, it is better, and more fun, with clues.

How did it all begin? Well, it was unintentionally and unknowingly conceived in the mid-nineteenth century by a Chagford man called James Perrot, a man of many talents, being a hunter, fisherman and walking guide. In this latter capacity he would take people who wanted to explore the remoter parts of Dartmoor to a boggy hollow in the wilderness known as Cranmere Pool. (Although it was once a pool, by the time Perrot was visiting it was empty.)

In 1854 he set up a cairn in this depression and placed a receptacle (a stone jar) inside it. Those few people who made the pilgrimage to this bleak spot were encouraged to leave their calling cards inside it for the next party to discover. Quite often this was weeks later. In the early twentieth century the jar was replaced by a more substantial box and as postcards were the standard means of passing messages on, those growing numbers of people visiting the pool were leaving them here for the next person to collect and post on. The improved box meant that a visitor's book could survive, despite the high amounts of rainfall. (Full books are housed in the Local Studies section of Plymouth City Library and are available for inspection.)

Thus 'letterboxing' began, albeit in its most primitive form. For more details of this genesis, please read *Cranmere Pool – The First Dartmoor Letterbox* by Chips Barber, also from Obelisk Publications.

"And There's More!"

As the years passed by other letterboxes were established, most of them, like Cranmere Pool, in out-of-the-way locations.

The boxes were not well hidden because the challenge lay in the walk to reach them, Ducks' Pool (1938), Fur Tor (1948), Sittaford Tor (1959) and Fish Lake (1968), being good examples of ones which demanded quite an expedition to collect the stamp. However, it wasn't until the 1970s that the 'letterbox boom' began. Now you would be hard-pressed to find a tor which does not have at least one box.

Letterboxes come in all shapes and sizes; they range from the metal ammunition tin, favoured by some for its robustness to withstand the harsh Dartmoor weather (but frowned upon by the Dartmoor National Park), to the more humble pill box dispensed by your chemist. In between there are various types of tins used and also the good-old tupperware container. All, bar Cranmere Pool and Ducks' Pool, will be hidden from view.

Nobody can say with any degree of accuracy how many 'letterboxes' are out on the moor at any one time but it could run to thousands. If this sounds excessive then you should consider that Dartmoor is a massive area, covering some 365 square miles, and the boxes themselves are extremely small! There is plenty of scope for hiding them.

A word of warning though … Letterboxing, as a hobby, can be very addictive and, once started, people have been known to spend every spare moment, whatever the weather, out on the moors in search of 'that elusive box'!

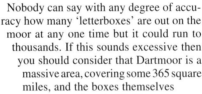

BELSTONE POST OFFICE

What the Well-Dressed Letterboxer is Wearing

It is not necessary to spend a fortune on specialist clothing as it's possible to find a great number of letterboxes within easy range of your parked vehicle, but it is important to understand the potentially dangerous environment that you will be 'boxing' in. Dartmoor demands respect and usually gets it, one way or another!

What you put on your feet is important – flip-flops will not do even on the finest of summer days and, although Wellington boots are often fine for a short outing, they are not suitable for longer excursions. Any self-respecting moorland walker should have footwear that is tough but comfy and which gives a degree of protection. It is almost inevitable that difficult terrain will be encountered. Dartmoor walking can be very hard on the feet and it can also be very soft!

Dartmoor's weather can be changeable, even in summer. Within minutes damp, penetrating mist can roll in from the Atlantic and turn what was a fine, warm day into something far less pleasant. It is important to be prepared for such a change of weather conditions so take something light, warm and weatherproof. Don't get caught out!

If you have no intention of going very far or staying out for very long, then you might not want to carry food and drink, but you should **never** walk without some emergency rations, particularly those which give energy and/or nourishment. Mint cake or glucose are good examples of 'food' that can revive flagging batteries when such situations arise.

There are certain items which are a must for any longer outing. A sensibly put together first aid kit to deal with tummy upsets, headaches, pains, cuts, stings, sunburn and so on can be light, compact and easily carried. If a longer expedition is planned, whistle, torch (with spare batteries) and survival bag are recommended items. And, I suppose, a sign of the times, a mobile phone can be useful in the event of a broken limb or some other emergency. The Dartmoor Rescue Group can be reached through the 999 number, but that would be only for the most serious situations.

An Ordnance Survey map of the area being walked, preferably 1:25000 (two and a half inches to the mile) is essential, as is a compass. However, the latter is no good unless you know how to use it properly!

So now you are, more or less, kitted out, what else do you need? An ink stamp pad (any colour will do), a hardback note book in which you can 'record' the letterbox stamps that you find (the firm back giving you a flat surface so that a good reproduction can be achieved) and a pen or pencil, just in case the ones in the 'boxes' that you find are missing.

Hungry

Letterbox

But Where Shall We Go Today?

Now that you have carefully prepared yourselves you will want to get started on this letterboxing adventure. There are several good starting places where you can not only enjoy the delights of Dartmoor but also find a few boxes, but

it's better not to be too ambitious at the outset. Here are three suggested locations where there are many boxes located within a mile of a car park.

There are at least seven Sharp Tors on the moor but the one near Dartmeet, high above the Dart Gorge, is the one where you could start your letterboxing. There is parking a few hundred yards from the tor, paths leading to this superb outcrop and the promise of several good boxes to find. Badger's Holt, at Dartmeet, is close by and sells refreshments – cream teas, ice creams and so on.

Haytor is probably the most famous rockpile on Dartmoor and because of this it has two large car parks and a Dartmoor information caravan sited in its lower one. Also, close by, there are toilets! A walk which embraces Saddle Tor, Haytor's near neighbour, should enable the letterbox seeker to find success. There are many boxes located on this part of the moor but there is also a lot of granite amongst which to hide them!

Another good place is Barn Hill, on the other, western, side of the moor, overlooking the Tavistock area. The car park, one of the biggest on the moor, is on the B3357 road from Tavistock to Princetown and situated at the top of Pork Hill, about a mile west of Merrivale. Again this area contains a great number of boxes but beware of not walking into the very damp and deep mire which lies below the impressive Vixen Tor! To avoid it you could perhaps use the Vixen Mire Passport as shown on the first page of this booklet. Many who establish letterboxes like to hide them where they can cover up the entrance with

other rocks. These can usually be spotted because they look different, or less natural, to the main rock under which they have been secreted. So if you spot a small pile of rocks stacked up against another larger one you have your starting place. Carefully move the smaller rocks aside and peer in. If you can see a box, take it out and examine what you have found. If you are lucky there should be a stamp, a book and, if you are fortunate enough to be the first to find it, there may also be a postcard for you to post back to the founder of the letterbox.

Now that you have found your first box you can stamp it in your own book, then add some witty comment to the 'visitors' book'. It's customary to write at least the date and your name. You may derive some pleasure, or even knowledge and wisdom, from reading the comments and observations of others who have found this box before you. Put everything carefully back in the box and return it to its hiding place ready for the next person to find. You can pat yourself on the back (always a tricky procedure) for being so clever as to find one. If you have children with you it will inevitably be them, with their energy and enthusiasm, who find it first.

The people who put out these boxes seem to come in two categories, those who wish them to be found easily and those who only want them discovered by those "in the know." The latter are known as "word of mouth" boxes and are usually very well hidden. Clues for these boxes are passed from boxer to boxer and are not generally available to all. It is amazing to meet people on the moor who ask you if you have this one or that one … and who then point a short distance away to one so cunningly concealed that you know you would never have had 'a cat in hell's' chance of finding it. However, these boxes aside, it is still possible to find many boxes just by searching around a rocky area or tor. So don't despair!

DON'T LET THEM DISAPPEAR

The more he looked, the more the letter wasn't there.

Please write soon.

What A Lot You Have Got (To Find)!

The placement of boxes is not as entirely random as it may appear at first to the novice boxer. It doesn't necessarily follow that the 'best' stamps are located in the most difficult positions. Boxes should not be placed in any location which is dangerous so you shouldn't need climbing gear or ropes to find them and you won't be expected to hang precariously over the top of a tor.

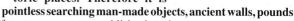

There is a code of conduct as to the siting of boxes, this having been established to protect important, sensitive and historic places. Therefore it is pointless searching man-made objects, ancient walls, pounds or enclosures like hut circles. If a person wants to establish a letterbox, like for instance to commemorate a particular person like poor Kitty Jay, it would be placed at a suitable and respectful distance away from her grave. The same working practice applies to ancient features like stone circles and so on. So don't waste your time by constantly walking over the ground of such important sites, you will draw blanks and, more importantly, you will damage the moor unnecessarily!

If you are new to Dartmoor and require a simple, but comprehensive overview of what it's all about then I can thoroughly recommend *The Great Little Dartmoor Book* by Chips Barber which will give you a good grounding, on most topics, for a modest outlay.

Every One A Winner

So, you have now found a few, maybe more than a few. Well done! If you flick through this booklet you will notice the range and diversity of letterbox stamps (because of limitations in space, most have been reduced in size, the originals being impressively large and expensive to create).

An appealing element of collecting letterbox stamps is the great variety of items portrayed in them. There are those which show the village stocks at Belstone, Totnes Guildhall, Chagford's 'Pepperpot' and many Dartmoor buildings.

It is also quite common to find different series of stamps put out on a theme or those which bear the images or caricatures of various personalities. Some have an obvious Dartmoor connection like Prince Charles, or William Crossing (1847–1928). He was a celebrated Dartmoor author who has a letterbox memorial at Ducks' Pool on Southern Dartmoor. But others like Ben Elton, Placido Domingo, Rory

Bremner, Gene Wilder, Michael Gambon, Lee Evans, Harold Wilson, Sigourney Weaver and Sylvester Stallone have no known appreciable moorland links, although now they are 'immortalised' in Dartmoor letterbox stamps!

Certain specific events have captured the imagination of those who have put out boxes: the Falklands conflict, the death of Princess Diana, the Tall Ships Race and so it goes on.

There are many memorial stamps. If one of your family or friends had a particular love of Dartmoor, or one favourite spot it is a lovely tribute to put out a box in their honour. But it is not just humans who are acknowleged in this fashion. Faithful pets, mainly cats and dogs, have had letterbox shrines established to their memory and it is a nice gesture to discover that the person responsible for placing it has supplied the box with dog biscuits or cat treats so that those who find it can take something home for their own pets.

There are many themes placed out on the moor and many hobbies and pastimes are reflected in the range which appear from time to time, for example, lovers of wildlife have set out letterbox trails on this theme so an ornithologist letterboxer can look for all the various wildbirds depicted on stamps, of which there are a great many.

Another letterbox concept is that of the charity walk designed to follow a trail, usually not too long, around a specific tor or area. This is designed to raise money for good causes and the boxer, in exchange for a few pounds, receives a set of clues to help find boxes put out on the moor for a limited time. Keep a look out in the windows of charity shops for details of such trails.

Finding Out More About Letterboxing

This hobby can be very relaxing; the joys of exploring a beautiful part of the moor can be very good for your body and soul. However it can be very frustrating when an elusive box that you have heard about, and that you have walked miles to find, is not found. After ages of looking, in all the likeliest of locations, without success, all you feel like doing is pulling your hair out! Probably the best thing to do is to become philosophical about it as, generally, boxing is a sociable and family-orientated hobby so it doesn't do to get too stressed about the non-appearance of a particular box. There's always another day and the chances are that you will meet someone who knows the precise spot where it is hidden and when you do go back you will probably kick yourself as you were so near but, oh so far, from finding it.

We have met many wonderful and friendly like-minded people out on the moor and have been invited to various letterbox get-togethers in Plymouth and other places. However the main meeting is held twice-yearly at the Dartmoor Prison Officers' social club in Princetown. The dates for this are easy to remember as the events, exactly six months apart, always coincide with 'the Changing of the Clocks', those two days of the year when we adjust our clocks forwards or back.

The person largely responsible for these immensely popular gatherings is Godfrey Swinscow, who has formed the totally unofficial '100 Club' which has accumulated some 12,000 members since it started many years ago. You become a 'member' after finding 100 letterboxes. Upon proving to Godfrey that you have visited said boxes, and having paid a small joining fee, he will send you a membership card and sew-on badge which you can wear or display with pride so that others can admire your achievement … until you see that they have their 200, 500, 1,000, 2,000 or even 3,000 badge! Then you will realise the scale and scope of the hobby which has consumed so many Dartmoor devotees.

'The Meet', as it is known, is a good place to chat and get to know other boxers. Many clues and secret boxes are disclosed and many boxers will produce one day stamps just for that particular 'Meet'. This is also the occasion where people will sell you the details of charity letterbox trails and a chance to buy other Dartmoor-related items such as books and equipment.

TOGETHER FOREVER

IAN + MERJE

OCTOBER 1998
39th Bi-Annual Meet
D.P.O.S.C.
PRINCETOWN

Mill Stone, Saddle Tor

Now What's Next?

Letterboxes are not confined to the Moor's 230 or so tors. They are found in a great variety of locations. Some of the more demanding ones are located at the heads of rivers, like those found where the Dart and Teign rivers rise. Many are located close to former industrial sites. The distinctive Wheal Betsy, an old engine house on the road from Tavistock to Okehampton, is one and the former gunpowder factory at Powder Mills between Postbridge and Two Bridges is another but there are many such industrial archaeological stamps. Many letterboxers have expanded their knowledge of the moor through finding, and then researching, boxes they have found so it's safe to say that this hobby is an educational one. If you find a box in need of attention, for instance saturated, contact the owner and/or the Letterbox 100 Club who will report the fact in the fortnightly updates.

Several of Dartmoor's public houses possess their own letterbox stamp, often installed in a box behind the bar. The Plume of Feathers at Princetown, the Dartmoor Inn at Merrivale and the Warren House on the road between Postbridge and Moretonhampstead are just three examples.

There are also several tourist attractions which host a stamp and these include the Bowden Museum, housed in Bowden's wonderful ironmonger's shop in Chagford, the Museum of Dartmoor Life in Okehampton and the Finch Foundry Museum at Sticklepath. If we included a list, which would be quite a long one, it would detract from the fun of finding them for yourself but as you can see we have given you a head start to get you going.

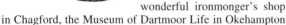

FINCH FOUNDRY MUSEUM

STICKLEPATH

The Cairn Fairy

The Rock Fairy

The River Fairy

The Plume of Feathers, Princetown
19 81
ICH DIEN
Royal Forest of Dartmoor

The Bowden Museum
CHAGFORD

I'd rather be 'boxing than .....

. . . riding a horse

BRIMPTS
FARM

BOX JANINE AND DONOVAN DOGGE'S 100

DR BLACKALL'S DRIVE

RUTHIE'S BOX

SCAREY TOR

LAIR SEEKER'S VIEWPOINT

It Takes All Sorts

People who 'letterbox' tend to have one thing in common – they do not take it too seriously and they like to have a bit of fun. This can be demonstrated. Most of us like to give ourselves silly names or some kind of persona so you may well come face to face with 'Hissing Sid', 'Dennis the Menace' or even 'Spiderman' in your moorland wanderings. When you have 'been in the business' for a while you will begin to notice familiar names cropping up time and again. It is also quite amazing to see where some of these letterboxers come from because we have seen addresses given from the USA, Japan and many other countries around the globe.

THE CHUDLEIGH WEALLS KITCHENS

Letterboxing has changed the lifestyles of many of those 'hooked' on the hobby. One entry in a visitors' book wrote, with an air of resign: *'We came for a quiet family holiday, and then my wife said "Let's start letterboxing!", so now we are out all day crawling around on hands and knees, but at least she is happy. I suppose I had better buy her a stamp of her own now.'*

Another typical entry stated: *'Freezing cold. Pouring rain. It's 8.00 a.m. I should be in bed. I must be off my head!'*

A number of personal stamps are shown here, ones you may care to look for when you are next out on the Moor. Some describe families like 'the Furneaux Five,' and 'the Four Foxes' from the Netherlands whilst others relate to their dogs like 'Sam & Duke'. Some appear to be obscure like 'Roomtrad' (think about it!), the 'Batty Bogger,' the 'Chudleigh Wealls' and so on. These roving letterboxers carry their personal stamps, known as 'Travellers', with them whilst exploring Dartmoor for boxes, so if you meet them, ask them for their personal stamp to add to your collection.

HAWKS TOR

Last But Not Least

As we have seen some boxes are established Dartmoor landmarks and have been there for a considerable time whilst others,'fly-by-nights', are put out for a short time, often for a particular reason. This means that the hobby is a never-ending one! One event that sees a large number of stamps put out on the moor each year is Christmas and it's not unusual for sixty or so festive letterbox greetings to appear. Perhaps a seasonal word of warning should be made here as it is largely children who are attracted by these boxes and their appearance coincides with the short, cold days of winter when night falls very quickly in the afternoon. Bearing in mind Dartmoor's reputation of being a mean and merciless moor at times great care and vigilance should be exercised when letterboxing with young children. It is better to avoid particularly wet areas, near mires, ponds or fast flowing rivers and streams.

As letterboxes are often placed in holes and as adders also like to live in similar habitats please take care when removing letterboxes, you don't want to find more than you bargained for. Although adder bites are not fatal, for most fit adults they can make you feel very ill so the use of a walking stick to poke around first is a tip we would like to pass on.

A large part of Northern Dartmoor is used by the military for training

purposes. There are three ranges, Okehampton, Willsworthy and Merrivale and when they are in use red flags are flown from many of the prominent high points within them. The edges of their territories are marked by red and white boundary markers. Before contemplating a letterbox walk on any or all of them it's worth checking first to see if they are in military use that day or night. The local press carry details on the Friday preceding any week, local police stations and post offices will have details and it's possible to get details by dialling 01837-52939. When you walk in these areas do **not,** repeat **not,** pick up any metal objects!

Please don't be put off by these final words of caution. Most letterboxers seem to go from adventure to adventure without too much bother and if you have read this carefully and acted upon the basic advice given you shouldn't have any problems either. And, although we are sure you will, please remember the Country Code also applies to Dartmoor so: Guard against all risk of fire; Fasten All Gates; Keep Your Dog on a Lead or Under Close Control; Keep to Paths across Farmland; Avoid Damaging Fences, Hedges and Walls; Leave No Litter; Safeguard Water Supplies; Protect Wildlife, Wild Plants and Trees.

We hope this book will help you to enjoy yourselves and we wish you happy and safe letterboxing!

BRADDON LAKE
DART COUNTRY
Gr. ref. 636796
Letterbox
established 1984
NORTHERN MOOR
Dartmoor National Park

No.27477

HORN'S CROSS

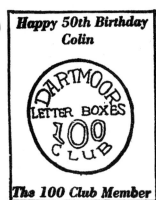

Happy 50th Birthday
Colin

DARTMOOR
LETTER BOXES
100
CLUB

The 100 Club Member

WALL PENNYWORT

Witchcraft &

Folklore

Redstart

"Coffin Stone"